MARTYN BREWSTER

Simon Olding

Martyn Brewster

With a foreword by Mel Gooding

SCOLAR PRESS

Published by
SCOLAR PRESS
Gower House
Croft Road
Aldershot
Hants GU11 3HR
England

Ashgate Publishing Company
Old Post Road
Brookfield
Vermont 05036-9704
USA

First published 1997

British Library Cataloguing in Publication Data
Olding, Simon
    Martyn Brewster
    1. Brewster, Martyn, 1952-   2. Painters – Great Britain –
    Biography 3. Painting, English 4. Painting, Modern – 20th
    century – Great Britain
    I. Title II. Brewster, Martyn, 1952-
    759.2

Library of Congress Catalog Card Number: 97-66328

Paperback ISBN 1 85928 439 6 (available only from the
Russell-Cotes Art Gallery and Museum)
Hardback ISBN 1 85928 414 0
Limited edition ISBN 1 85928 415 9

Produced for the publishers by
John Taylor Book Ventures
Hatfield, Herts
Designed by Alan Bartram
Typeset in Bembo by Nene Phototypesetters, Northampton
Printed in Great Britain by Offset Southampton

Frontispiece and illustration on page 93: photographs by Hattie Miles

Cover/jacket illustrations:
Front: *Beauty and Sadness*, No.10, oil on canvas 1996
Back: *Lowick*, No.450, silkscreen monoprint 1996

Published on the occasion of
the exhibition *Martyn Brewster*
at the Russell-Cotes Art Gallery and Museum, Bournemouth
Opening June 1997

A limited edition of 50 copies, numbered and signed by the artist, includes a multicoloured unique silkscreen monoprint.

Contents

Author's acknowledgements

I should like to thank a number of people who have made significant contributions to this study. Martyn himself has been a kind and helpful critic of the text, ensuring its accuracy, and Mark Bills has made pertinent comments. I particularly want to thank Diane Edge for her important contribution to the production of the book and Jill George for her unfailing support of this project. A catalyst for writing was the retrospective exhibition held at the Russell-Cotes Art Gallery and Museum, Bournemouth from 1997 and then touring to galleries in England. The Arts Council of England's development grant to research the exhibition and potential venues was particularly valuable and a special mention must be made of James Howe's remarkable photographs as well as the photographic contribution made by Martyn Brewster, Hattie Miles and Graham Bush, Sue Ormerod, Rodney Todd-White and Paul Morris.

The author dedicates the book to Jane Baker.

Artist's acknowledgements

For Bob, Doreen, Simon and Sophie Brewster and dedicated to the memory of my Grandmother.

It would be almost impossible to name all the family, friends, writers, teachers and students who have helped me over the years; they know who they are, and I am very grateful for their support. I would like to thank the teaching and technical staff I have worked with at Bournemouth and Poole College of Art and Design, particularly Mike Rees, and also Dr Jan Krir and Alan Jones for helping me make a 'new life' in Dorset. I have enjoyed staying at the Lowick House Print Workshop and I am indebted to John and Margaret Sutcliffe for giving me the opportunity to work there on a number of occasions recently. I would also like to thank Mel Gooding for his perceptive introduction, and Mark Bills for his constant assistance throughout this project. Most of all I wish to express my gratitude to Simon Olding and Jill George for making this book possible.

Foreword

The art of Martyn Brewster takes its place within two great histories. The first is the grand and complex tradition of European Romantic and post-Romantic landscape painting. This contains within it (to identify elements that can be seen to have fed most directly into Brewster's work) the great and radical breakthroughs to expressivity of Turner and Constable, the densely atmospheric realism of Courbet, the brilliant efflorescences of French Impressionism and post-Impressionism, including the late Monet of the lily pond paintings, and the psychologically-charged colourism of Northern artists such as Caspar David Friedrich, van Gogh, Nolde, and de Staël. The second is the dynamic and richly complicated phenomenon of post-war painterly abstraction, with its interplay of American and European developments, its spiritual and mythic pretensions on the one hand, its claims to expressive authenticity on another, its intent to a symbolic transformation of the visible world on a third, and its ambition, in all those cases, to achieve a self-contained objective autonomy. It is true, of course, that in some of its manifestations this latter line has grown out of the former, and that many of the underlying themes that animated nineteenth- and early twentieth-century landscape painting have found their modern expression in non-figurative art.

This is not to suggest that Brewster is essentially a landscape painter, for he has followed a resolutely principled course in non-figuration, making paintings (and prints) that insist upon their material self-sufficiency, so to speak, as objects in the world rather than as pictures of the world. But it is certainly the case that until recently there has persisted in his work a great deal of reference to natural phenomena, frankly registered in the titles he gives his paintings. In *Early Light* (1986, ill.31), the pale creamy yellow that predominates in the upper two-thirds of the painting recalls the early morning light of those late Turners in which all things are dissolved to a misty-luminous immateriality; *Scent of Rain* (1986, ill.34) catches the aerial disturbance of a summer shower with its scattered refractions of floral colour, its freshening of the brilliant air; *Lakeside III* (1986) and *Catching the Light* (1992) play in quite different ways with the contrast of bright reflected light and deep shadow.

There is a simple evocative poetry in those titles (as also in *In the Garden*, 1986, *Fire and Water*, 1991, *Falling Light*, 1992, *The Great River*, 1992, etc) which at times hardly matches the blazing intensities of colour and textural furore that characterise the paintings themselves. They read, rather, as afterthoughts, nominations suggested by some aspect of a finished work that itself bears the evidences of procedures that have purposes more complex than the transcription of the visible. Even so, as one painting follows another, there is the cumulative acknowledgement in their titles that if they do not directly picture the natural world, they may be seen to reflect its atmospheres and colours, its densities and vagueness, its brilliant variegations. Brewster's poetic abstraction begins with the experience of natural objects (focused and intensified, as we know, by a continuous practice of drawing from the motif) and ends with images analogous with things seen and felt in nature.

Freed of the requirement of description, evocative non-figuration of this kind can go beyond reflecting the visible, representing a view of a landscape or imitating the look of things; it may, 'above all,' in August Strindberg's words, 'imitate the manner in which nature creates'. In so doing, painting can recreate for the viewer the sensation of being-in-nature, of experiencing the natural world in its momentum, its unceasing inter-penetration of time, space, objects and the body. In certain titles Brewster proposes this phenomenological experience as the 'subject' of the work: in *Above and Beyond*, the great triptych of 1986 (ill.33), a stupendous sequence of high verticals creates successive moments of cosmic turmoil in what might be deep sky or deep water; *Moving Through* (1992) may record the fleeting glimpses we have of things as we move through the landscape, or register the blue-white blur of something other passing across the crammed space into which we are looking; *Into the Night* (1992) proposes a darkening, a condition of in-between-ness as the light dies and colour is eclipsed. These sensations are invoked by colour that is always complicated by inflection, that flickers like colour-light in day-time, or vibrates like night's dark, its blacks, pierced by points of light, deepening at dusk or fading and paling at dawn. They are intensified by a substantial actuality of paint that presents itself tactile to the eye, its variations of slabby smoothness and turbulent impasto catching the light in an infinite variety of effects as the eye pursues its unpredictable trajectories across the canvas surface.

The imagined adventures of the senses to which these paintings invite us are not un-like those we might enjoy in front of a Constable, whose broken surfaces were the first to catch at the flicker of nature in that way, by means of facture rather than by illusionistic *trompes*; or in contemplation of the late lily pond paintings of Monet in which we ex-perience the simultaneous, and contradictory, sensations of scanning across the horizontal surface of the pool and looking into its depths, only to realise as we emerge from the reverie they induce that our gaze has been intent upon an opaque vertical surface, an object on the wall of a room. The structurings of sumptuous colour that are typical of the paintings Brewster made at the beginning of the 1990s, rough rectangles of hot crimson, scarlet, green, orange, distributed within a more generalised field that suggests natural space, or in the smaller *Variation series* (ill.42-45) simply abutting one another as if jostling for the limited space available, may also remind us of de Staël, whose work at the edge of figuration and non-figuration dramatised for the post-war European generation the dilemma between stylised representation and abstraction from nature. Brewster's work comes to its recollections of de Staël from the opposite direction to that of the master: it begins in colouristic abstraction and a feeling for nature, and ends on the edge of landscape; and it never goes over.

All this is not a matter of what are usually described as 'influences'. It has to do, rather, with the connections and continuities that enable us to characterise the nature and par-ticularity of Brewster's achievement, and to identify its place in the historical discourse of painting. Any painter working today in a mode of gestural abstraction, and having the ambition and courage to essay the sublime in modern terms, which is to say through colour and painterly forms rather than through an imagery of spectacular landscapes, of mountains, sea and sky, must work with an awareness of the self-conscious heroics of New York painting in its most ambitious phase.

(Brewster is also a gifted and inventive printmaker, but his efforts in that field parallel his work as a painter; what is true of the paintings in terms of their historical ante-cedents, their characteristic mood and thematic drift, is to a great extent true of the prints, the more so in that so much of Brewster's graphic output takes the form of monoprints, which by definition are individual works, and bear the imprint of direct intervention in the realisation of the final image. What is more, in most cases they take up and improvise themes treated serially in concurrent paintings.)

Thus there can be discerned in Brewster's work, confidently assimilated to a personal manner that is unmistakably his own, visible traces of Hans Hofmann (that opposition of hard-edge geometric forms to freely-painted and disturbed spatial fields already remarked in the paintings of 1991-92: a strategy exploited to brilliant effect in paintings made in the mid- to late-1970s by John Hoyland, an artist much admired by Brewster); of De Kooning (the ambiguous landscape-like spatialities and vivid atmospherics of paintings like *In the Garden*, 1986, ill.32, and *Ocean Light*, 1990, ill.39); and, most noticeably in the *Beauty and Sadness* paintings of 1996 (ill.48,50-52,64), of Clyfford Still (the density and immensity of dark planes with rents of light and bright colour breaking through at the edges) and Rothko (the horizontal division of the image, atmospheric soft-edged blocks of colour). Brewster draws upon the exalted idioms of Abstract Expressionism – he is too intelligent an artist not to be keenly aware of these affiliations and affinities – in order to power his own utterance: his conversation with American painting is conducted in his own voice, and with a Northern European rather than an English inflection.

In fact, Brewster's painting, in particular its chromatic intensity and factural drama, can be seen as most directly related in spirit and mood to the various manifestations of expressive romanticism and Symbolism that dominated German and Scandinavian painting at the turn of the century and after. Lyrical, dramatic, contemplative by turns, such painting, exemplified in the landscapes of Munch, Prince Eugen, Strindberg, and, later, Nolde, and having a crucial antecedence in Friedrich, is the outcome of a deeply meditated engagement with landscape and with what Wordsworth called 'natural objects'. It finds in the phenomenal world of fire and air, earth and water, external correlatives for internal thought and feelings. This discovery of nature, as itself reflective of the contemplating mind and its emotions, is something quite distinct from the recognition of the charm, beauty or grandeur of lake, river, waterfall, mountain, early light, ocean light, winter light, nightfall, lightfall, and their effective picturing for the delight of others. It is a philosophical project conducted by the poetic means of analogy and metaphor, and incorporating the hazards that individuate things or create the infinite variety of events in the experienced world: this is what Strindberg meant by a 'new art … the art to come', that which will imitate not the forms of nature but 'the manner in which nature creates'.

Brewster's mode of organic abstraction begins with the random mark on the canvas, itself an event in nature, and moves through stages in which colour and texture are successively built up and destroyed; procedures of working informed by a complex of recollection, intuition, choice and chance. This dynamic play with the materials of his art, paint and glaze laid into the plane of the canvas, creates an image that is at once an evocation of objective natural phenomena and an expressive sign for subjective experience. In a note on his most recent work Brewster himself draws an interesting distinction between the paintings in which the former predominates, those 'Nature' paintings which 'reflect a more overt concern with movement and light, the world out there', and those in which an abstract equivalence is found for interior thoughts and emotions, works reflecting 'a quieter, meditative and melancholic concern'. Brewster knows that in either case the basis of his art is phenomenological. For the invention of the abstract languages of modernist painting has removed the necessity for the description of the outward forms and moods of nature, and made possible an art like his own that draws upon the deepest personal experience of the hidden dynamics of things, finding continuities between the energies that animate external nature and those that move the heart to joy and suffering.

What is seen is part of the eye that sees it, the mind that conceives it, the spirit which celebrates it, the emotion that responds to it. Whether or not he would subscribe in a conscious or critical way to this essentially Kantian subjectivism, there can be no doubt that Brewster sees his work as having the power to transcend, as in a ceremony, the dichotomy of subject and object: 'In essence,' Brewster writes, 'all the works are celebratory whether or not they are more concerned with an intense interest in what we see "out there" or what we feel "inside"'. And of the paintings in the *Beauty and Sadness* series, whose very title spans the divide between what is perceived and what is felt, he hopes that 'their stillness is suffused with atmosphere' – the weather and mood of nature – 'and vibrant with longing' – the affections of the experiencing subject. Remembering the title of a 1990 painting, we may say that all his works are 'heart songs', their words and music found in correspondence to the effects of nature.

The emotive intensity of his work, the psychological density of his colourism, the expressive range of his handling of paint, the variety and richness of its answer to the elements and aspects of the received world: these are the things that mark Brewster out as very much his own man in the contexts of contemporary painting. His work lacks the ironies, reflexive, existential or satirical, that complicate so much modern painting; it does not say one thing and mean another, or try to say nothing at all. Its complications are of another order. Its constant play with darkness and light, the dramatic contrasts of its chromatic vibrancies and bituminous complex blacks, its lyrical atmospherics, its translucencies and opacities, these are the components of a symbolic language that aspires to the vitality and complexity necessary to the expression of a passionate and vigorous poetic imagination.

MEL GOODING January 1997

Strindberg's manifesto on modern art, *Des Arts Nouveaux! ou Le hasard dans la production artistique* ('On New Art, or Chance in artistic production') was published in Paris in 1894. It is quoted in the catalogue of the Arts Council of Great Britain's exhibition of Scandinavian painting at the turn of the century, 'Dreams of a Summer Night', at the Hayward Gallery, London, 1986. Examples of works by Strindberg, and by Prince Eugen and Munch, are reproduced in the catalogue. Kant discusses the subjective nature of the sublime in Part I, Book II, of the 'Critique of Pure Judgment'. Martyn Brewster is quoted from the catalogue of his exhibition, 'Beauty and Sadness', at the Jill George Gallery, London, 1996. The title 'Beauty and Sadness' is taken from a novel by the Japanese writer Yasunari Kawabata.

Martyn Brewster by Simon Olding

Context and influences

Martyn Brewster's studio is on the upper floor of a building situated at the end of his garden in Boscombe, Bournemouth. The space is neatly and professionally organised, works in progress stacked carefully along one wall, a series of small oil paintings meticulously arranged along another. The studio has an intensely private character, but it also shows signs of thoughtful organisation and a dignified planning amongst the sumptuous array of colourful canvases and working photographs. The studio is a space of peace, observance, and high discipline. The artist's methods of working, too, emphasise these important qualities. The day's work of painting takes place against the background of carefully selected music. This musical accompaniment – a string quartet by Schubert, a composition by Miles Davis – will give order and inspiration to the task of painting. The approach is cool, analytical. Yet the paintings themselves are passionate, romantic and richly suffused with colour. Brewster himself would see no contradiction in this disciplined approach which yields such poetic results. He is determined, driven even, by a profound need to express his emotional and intellectual concerns through art. In dedicating himself to this task, with its requirements for long periods of still reflection and lonely work, he can seem self-absorbed, guarding his privacy. By nature something of a loner, he expresses views of sometimes boundless joy and optimism through his work. A private man, his work shares with others a conviction in the beauty and solace of both nature and great art.

The signature of Martyn Brewster's work – whether in acrylic, oil, screenprint or artist's book – is colour. This survey shows that he has held, with something akin to a moral certainty, an extraordinary conviction that nature and emotion can be passionately conveyed by organising vivid, exuberant, and most recently, sombre areas of colour on to rectangular or square canvases or paper. Brewster has followed a long-term plan to paint lyrically and often romantically with colour. His creative purpose has not been pursued at the whim of fashion, homage to other styles, or genuflection to art history. Nor is this a recipe for tired re-workings of a once compelling, but now hackneyed idea. Brewster works in a virtuoso way through his chosen plan. He is equally skilled at painting in oil on canvas, acrylic on paper, or working in the print studio. The idea of painting works in series has led to an excursion into the production of the artist's book, with fine rewards.

If Brewster's work is characterised by rich colour, then an attendant feature is the energy and dynamism with which paint is used. In *Wildfire* (1994, oil on canvas, ill.46) a small, square, oil painting sits hardly contained within its sombre matt black frame. A passionate and closely worked red backdrop draws the viewer's eye to a blazing chasm at the heart of the canvas. Around it, as if in turmoil, spasms of blue, green and yellow paint have been frenziedly applied to the surface of the picture. It is as if they are held in a momentary freezing of time before being drawn into the fiery heart. The work is an intense evocation, perhaps of a mood, perhaps of the imagining of some geological or atmospheric process. The decorative effect is achieved entirely through the skilled handling of saturated colour. Seen as a single work, *Wildfire* has an immediate intensity. Seen as part of the series from which it derives (series number 55, square variations) the work has a more allusive identity. Brewster can sustain this level of energy of work in the series, because he has such a coherent plan for that work. This study of his career demonstrates consistency, seriousness of resolve, and a powerful concentration. These are attributes which have led Brewster to achieve considerable success, as well as sustaining him during his life's mission to paint.

Keith Patrick, in an important essay on Martyn Brewster's work for the catalogue accompanying an exhibition at Jill George's Thumb Gallery in 1990, draws attention to Brewster's steadfast view of abstraction, which has remained a feature of the artist's work since student days in Brighton. Patrick says that Brewster's 'faithfulness to abstraction … when the prevailing fashion had turned elsewhere' was a mark both of the artist's maturity and his singular determination. He points out that Brewster's student work in lyrical abstraction was undertaken when successive fashions for Pop, Op, Minimal and Conceptual art had apparently consigned such colour painting to critical obscurity. Patrick argues that his work should be seen in a British romantic landscape tradition. This tradition of nature painting, starting with the works of Turner and Constable, and influencing the neo-romantics in Britain painting in the 1930s and 1940s, is marked by an element of disillusionment with the materialism of urban life. Brewster's direct engagement with nature, and the emotions inspired by natural forces, may be seen in a historical context. Other commentators have reflected on the artist's debt to Monet, particularly in his largest nature paintings, and emphasised the influences of John Hoyland's powerful, vibrant abstract paintings as well as Dennis Creffield's expressive and occasionally violent work. Inevitably critics have placed Brewster's work squarely in the tradition of Abstract Expressionism.

These are convenient shorthands for an understanding of Martyn Brewster's colour paintings. Such observations help us to find a route into an understanding of his vivid, urgent and richly coloured work. The artist would not claim for a moment that his work has not been influenced in some manner, by inspired teachers, or by his own personal artistic preferences; but he has, despite clear influences, developed his own distinctive voice. This has not been a cold or heartless crusade; Brewster's method of working is creative, not careerist. As a number of critics have pointed out, the role of the lyrical abstract painter has been a lonely one, but this is the territory from which Brewster has chosen his inspiration. If he is compelled to paint from nature, or driven by emotional circumstances to produce works of often passionate beauty using the force of abstract colour as a guiding principle, then it has proved to be a life's work of commanding strength and integrity. Throughout Brewster's painting career we can see a determination to pursue the chosen end point of abstract colour painting. There have been no radical shifts of direction in this plan. Technical skill and a fierce eye for organisation and form have always been hallmarks of his work. So this is a study of conviction and certainty as well as of lyrical beauty. Brewster himself has achieved that rare thing, creativity without compromise, and continued to find commercial success. These are fitting tributes to the vitality of his work and its relevance through the shifting sands of contemporary fashions in fine art.

Early works

Martyn Brewster was born in 1952 in Oxford, moving with his parents, his younger
brother and grandmother to Watford when he was 10. Both Martyn's parents were gifted
craftspeople. His father, Bob, was a classically trained bookbinder, working at the Oxford
University Press and later teaching bookbinding and printing techniques in Oxford.
The family's move to Watford in 1962 was as a result of a successful application for a new
teaching post at Watford Technical College. Martyn remembers being disconcerted at
the move and found it difficult at first to settle into his new life with its change of school
and friends. His mother, Doreen, also excelled in craft skills and was well known for her
excellence in embroidery and design. Brewster had a settled and happy childhood, and
his parents were very supportive of both of their sons' aspirations to go to Art School.
Simon, Martyn's brother, trained at Ravensbourne Art College in fine art, and today
jointly runs a successful graphic design business. Martyn learned perfectionism and
patience as well as determination and resolution from his parents. He owes a particular
emotional debt to his grandmother who lived with the family until she died in 1972,
aged 93. She had a calming and dignified influence on the family life. Martyn's deep

1. *Standing figure.*
Charcoal on paper 1971.
23 × 16½

2. *Seated nude.*
Charcoal on paper 1972.
30½ × 20½

affection was to be given powerful visible evidence in an influential series of portraits of his grandmother made during his early years as an artist. Brewster learned to value self-respect as well as respect for others from his settled and warm family life. His quiet, somewhat retiring and conventional family upbringing have left their marks of determination and shyness on the artist today.

His parents were very pleased by their son's intention and desire to go to Art School. The high academic aspirations of Watford Boys Grammar School would have created some pressure, as it did on all pupils, to put academic distinction and intellectual achievement above other skills, and the school measured its success in terms of the number of students going on to study at Oxbridge. However, Brewster found, alongside an aptitude for sport, that his vocation was in the fine arts. His first art teacher, Jim Smith, through his warm and considerate personality, helped to draw the young artist out of himself. Brewster, painfully shy as a young man, responded positively to Smith's kindness and warmth, feeling that he had found genuine understanding in the somewhat authoritarian atmosphere of the school. The art class became a familiar place of contentment, and a secure base from which to learn and to test out new skills in drawing and composition. After his A-level years, he was successful in gaining a place at the then St Alban's School of Art and Design (now Hertfordshire College). The foundation year reinforced his determination to succeed in his chosen career as a painter. He commuted daily to the newly created school by train, and hardly mixed with his fellow students, so determined was he to work hard and diligently. Brewster recalls this as a crucial and influential year. He responded to the intense training as well as the painterly and expressive teaching that took place at the school, reacting warmly to the serious, disciplined and vigorous atmosphere which set him on a course to paint which he has since followed with utter determination.

Martyn Brewster's earliest paintings (1968 to 1973) show, as might be expected from a student searching for his first artistic voice, a variety of styles and finishes. They vary from the first canvas of 1968-69, *Untitled* (ill.13), with its angular oppositions of white and demodulated brown, interspersed with flecks and lines of red, to the more whimsical and figurative *Dancing Nun* of 1972. Included in this period are purely representational works such as *Bedroom in Brighton* (ill.17) with its rather Euston Road School feeling of a downcast student lodging. Other representational paintings in their stiff manner clearly show the artist endeavouring to triumph over technique, rather than being led by the passion of a visual idea. Much of this early period was spent drawing, especially from the figure and landscape, under a succession of inspiring teachers. Brewster warmly acknowledges his debts to Jim Smith, his school art teacher, followed by Arnold Van Praag, Roger Leworthy and Dennis Creffield at Art School. But it was not long before Brewster began to find his own voice and form. Self-portraits, and a powerful small study of his Grandmother from 1971, when Brewster was concluding his first formal period of training, show an artist of undoubted technical skill exploring and experimenting with a variety of subjects and styles.

To describe Brewster's artistic development as a systematic programme of painting may sound unemotional. Whilst the body of work shows clear evidence of planning, singularity and purpose, often expressed in related series of works, this painting project is one which encapsulates and orders emotion. Emotion, passion and a personal view of nature are not driven out of these canvases, they are effectively contained and regulated within

3   4

them. What is remarkable is the speed with which Brewster moved towards a highly coherent and systematic vision of painting. Throughout his early training, at the Hertfordshire College of Art and Design (1970-71) and at Brighton Polytechnic, where he took a first class degree in fine art, followed by a postgraduate painting and printmaking award (with distinction) at the Polytechnic in 1974-75, Brewster demonstrated a rapid focus and move towards his chosen medium of colour abstract painting. Indeed there is a discernible moment in 1973 towards the end of his first degree course at Brighton Polytechnic where the language of his paintings changed discernibly and previous experimentations in styles and the use of differing materials became clearly focused.

These first art school and student paintings are, as one would expect, intensely private works, not intended for public display. They show a range of styles and experiments with paint from the purely abstract to the representational. What is common to these works is the confident handling of paint demonstrated in particular in the 1971 painting *Grandmother* (ill.16) and a self-portrait dating from 1972 (ill.22). The self-portrait shows the artist looking at himself grimly and with a deadpan gaze. The work has something of the bold use of colour and strident handling of paint characterised by works of Emil Nolde,

3. *Garden, Hertfordshire.*
Charcoal on paper 1973.
30 × 20

4. *Garden series*, No.4
(The tall tree).
Etching ed.60 1993. 8 × 6

15

whereas the study of his Grandmother is a frank but more figurative study of a close
family member caught somewhat unprepossessingly asleep in a favourite Victorian arm-
chair. The portraits of Brewster's grandmother in the early part of the foundation year
at Art School mark a small but significant turning-point. His teachers proposed that he
undertake a more directly personal painting project in order to test his capabilities. He
responded with a series of works in oil and drawing of his much-loved Grandmother
which met the challenge and stretched the artist's technical and imaginative capabilities.
A more impressionistic style is captured in the oil painting *The Blossom Trees* (1971,
ill.18), a vital study of a cherry tree in full blossom from an ordinary suburban street at
his parent's home in Watford, buffeted by wind yet standing proudly and firmly as the
focus at the centre of the painting.

Other works from this period continue to demonstrate Brewster's desire to investigate
modes and methods of painting in order to determine the beginnings of his own particular artistic voice. These student works also include heads, as well as the witty oil painting
Dancing Nun (1972) which depicts a faceless woman against a hard and flat background,
ironically caught in Marilyn Monroe's famous pose in the film *The Seven Year Itch* with

5. *Devil's Dyke, Sussex.*
Ink pen and wash 1978.
11½ × 16

16

6. *Welsh landscape.*
Ink and wash 1985. 12 × 17

her skirt blowing around her waist. These early paintings demonstrate a knowledge and understanding of other current artistic movements which Brewster was eventually able to reject confidently in favour of his own form of lyrical abstraction. He began to sell work as early as 1970, during his first year at Hertfordshire College of Art and Design.

The early oil paintings of still lifes with fish and fruit show a confident handling of form, as well as an immediate skill in drawing. They are confident and comfortable, rather than challenging, works. Perhaps among the most interesting paintings of this period is a series of portraits of friends and family, in particular the stark and colourful pictures of Brewster's grandmother. Some of these works, including the lyrical and more softly coloured portrait of *Paula Harler* (1972), were commissioned, and are often characterised by intense and impassively still studies of the sitter's face and silent gaze.

Brewster moved to Brighton after his foundation year in St Albans. He had taken a trip to the town to see friends, feeling somewhat at a loss as to which Art School to apply to for the next stage in his training. Whilst in Brighton he visited an exhibition by Dennis Creffield at the Gardner Arts Centre, and was powerfully impressed by the work. He applied to Brighton Polytechnic on the strength of this exhibition, believing that the possibility of training with Creffield would prove inspirational. Creffield was indeed to become Brewster's tutor and a powerful influence. He epitomised an expressionist and painterly approach to handling colour, and his strong charcoal drawings were particularly compelling. This work struck a deep chord with Brewster, who found that it gave direction and energy to his own paintings; but whilst acknowledging his debt to Creffield, he was strong willed and determined enough not to slavishly follow his teacher's line, but to use it to discover in himself his own individual voice and style, and to paint in a more abstract manner.

An oil painting of the artist's long-standing friend Mark Gallagher (1972, ill.19) shows the artist's internal struggle for style. With something of the relaxed yet shapely handling of form and paint in Claude Rogers' portraits, it is essentially a humorous and kindly work, very different in character from other, chilling, self-portraits. Brewster's figure paintings from life classes at Brighton Polytechnic have a more impassioned use of colour than these portrait studies. The handling of paint becomes freer, and the forms of the figure and the studio are abstracted, releasing an energy in the use of the paint on the canvas. There is something of the style of 'model in studio' paintings by Pierre Bonnard in these early works, but what is most apparent is the move towards painting in an abstract or semi-abstract style. This was largely the result of painting from drawings rather than, as previously, working directly from the model. This gradually became a preferred means of working since it allowed him to abstract from the figure to a much greater extent, to move images around, and to use colour in a more subjective manner. This mode developed during 1974 as Brewster was concluding his first degree in painting at the Polytechnic.

At this point Brewster was offered a place on Harvey Daniel's postgraduate printmaking course at the Polytechnic, an offer which was to prove extremely influential for his future career. Brewster learned rapidly and enthusiastically the techniques of silkscreen printing and etching. He had an inspirational year, feeling strongly that his place on the course gave a seal of recognition at exactly the right time in his development and opened up opportunities for printmaking which might not have come without being on the course. Enterprisingly, Brewster also found the time and resources to continue with his painting, hiring a modest studio in Brighton.

In 1975, leaving Brighton Polytechnic with a postgraduate printmaking diploma with distinction, Brewster felt that he had had his fill of formal art institutions. He spent over a year working in the Brighton Open Studios, a group of teachers and artists sharing studio space and organising exhibitions each year. Here he continued painting alongside printmaking, enjoying for the first time the mutual support of a small and closely knit group of artists, and undertaking, as necessary, labouring and other jobs to support himself in between periods of unemployment. He also took the opportunity in these years to travel to Europe with friends, to see museums and galleries in Spain, Italy and France.

In 1977, Brewster again found that his career and life were to change direction. He had met Hilary Carter, his future wife, a trained infant teacher, and many of his friends had moved on to London. Increasingly uncertain how to earn a living he decided to take the postgraduate teaching certificate place that he had held over for two years, and gained an art teacher's certificate at Sussex University in 1978.

Brewster's paintings from 1973 to 1980 concentrate on colour abstraction, and indicate the beginnings of his mature style. This was the period during which he concluded his formal education at Brighton Polytechnic, winning a highly-regarded Eastern Arts award in 1977. Photographs of Brewster's diploma show for Brighton Polytechnic demonstrate the vitality and strength of his charcoal drawings as well as the vigour of his work in oil. For a young man of twenty-two to produce such a coherent and striking body of work, showing equal facility in drawing and painting, demonstrates an early maturity as well as the beginnings of a commitment to a predictable and passionately felt style of painting. Works from this period fall into two distinct groups. A number of paintings depict lines of moving figures, with human forms merged into a seething crowd where only the mass of people can be discerned, rather than individual features or faces. This series can be read in two ways; either as abstracts, or as semi-representational studies of crowd scenes. The palette is more neutral than highly coloured, though this is not a feature of his purely abstract paintings from the same period.

This second group of intensely coloured abstract paintings shows the influence of works by David Bomberg, the American Abstract Expressionists, and the St Ives painters, in particular Peter Lanyon. An oil, *Autumn* (1974, ill.24), is a turbulent expression of thickly layered paint on canvas with strident areas of red contrasting with heavily worked whites and browns across an energised canvas. A more dispassionate approach is taken in other oil paintings where blocks of deep blues, reds and greens are arranged in a more organised manner on the canvas, in the style of de Staël or Hans Hofmann. It is from these works that we can begin to see the development of Brewster's mature style. The careful organisation of colour, and a move to pure abstraction have become the identifying feature of his painting from this period although the debt to Hofmann is occasionally too literal. A few works play with the notion of a canvas grounded with dark colours, interspersed with sparse areas of more intense colour. The idea of these paintings was to lie dormant until the mature expression of the 1990s in paintings within the *Beauty and Sadness* series (ill.48,50–52,64). The line that can be drawn between these works, spanning twenty years of creative production, indicates the seriousness of Brewster's resolve to paint within a particular and carefully chosen style of colour abstraction. His interest in the lyrical use of paint, and in the submerging of representation into a semi-abstract canvas become themes which are worked out and developed during this early period. Brewster found his voice as an artist very quickly.

Developing the style

The 1980s were a defining decade for the artist, when his work developed into its mature style. Having lived in Brighton during most of the 1970s he now moved with Hilary Carter to Walthamstow in north-east London. Brewster began to combine his career as a serious painter with that of professional teacher, undertaking posts as lecturer in art at the East Hertfordshire College, Cheshunt (1980–89), and securing an important post as visiting lecturer at the Winchester School of Art. These posts gave him more stability and focus than he had ever known before, as well as a valuable income. He worked a four-day week teaching, painting at his studio at home in Walthamstow at the weekends, finding that a degree of economic control helped his work to blossom and gain maturity. In 1986 Brewster, feeling more confident and settled in his emotional and professional life, took the risk of leaving full-time teaching by establishing a job-share post at East Hertfordshire College. The new part-time post gave Brewster significantly more time to paint, and his work flourished. He began to sell more work, and from this point has never returned to full-time teaching. He also acquired a large studio at Britannia Works, one of the SPACE Studios in Hackney, from where he was able easily and regularly to visit galleries and exhibitions throughout London.

The late 1980s were a period of considerable fulfilment in both his professional and personal life, with regular exhibitions held at Jill George's Gallery in Soho from 1987, and the birth of Brewster's daughter Sophie in 1988. Martyn and Hilary also felt that the time was propitious to consider at least a part-time move out of London. They bought a small house in Bournemouth in 1988 having been attracted to the area as a result of visiting friends in Dorset. By the end of the 1980s Brewster's time was divided between Bournemouth and London. He was successful in finding a part-time teaching post at the Bournemouth and Poole College of Art and Design in 1989 and continued to divide his time between his studio in London and a newly acquired studio in Bournemouth. The move to Dorset was to prove inspirational.

The studio in Bournemouth gave him a new grounding and direction, and his teaching commitments at the Art College proved to be stimulating and enjoyable. He made contact with a number of well-known Dorset-based artists at the College including Jim Hunter, Brian Bishop, Eddy Foulstone, Brian Graham and Peter Joyce. However, for all of these professional benefits, this was a difficult period for Brewster; there were personal and emotional difficulties. The move out of London could not mask tensions and difficulties that he was experiencing in his marriage.

A signature painting such as *Above and Beyond* (oil on canvas, 1986, ill.33) clearly demonstrates the creative authority of work from this period. What is immediately obvious is the confident manner in which Brewster handled his large canvas. The use of the diptych and triptych now become a feature, requiring the additional skill of presenting a coherent and organised work across multiple canvases. Brewster accepted this challenge with alacrity. His skill in creating pictures with grand internal narratives, and over large spaces, is a mark not only of competence, but also of the rich creative seam of ideas flowing into his works during the 1980s.

Above and Beyond is a painting of majestic scope. Its title may refer to a particular natural circumstance – looking into a deep blue sea, or looking at an intense night sky. The purpose of the painting seems to accommodate both perspectives. It is a poem about the natural world, and the way in which we inhabit the earth, both as physical and metaphysical beings. This canvas cannot, then, be contained by a view of one place at one time. The organisation of the painting into three distinct but related panels reinforces this view of narrative, and the requirement of each individual to merge subtly differing views about their relationship with nature at different times and in different places. Brewster's work has become a completely abstracted view of the possibility of thinking intensely about natural phenomena. Across each of the deep blue canvases, a hurriedly worked lighter blue 'cloud' passes across the painting from left to right scored with, first, a block, and then flecks, of bright red. The effect is one of a journey of colour, of colour having a physical force and movement. This is a work of commanding scale and complete conviction, and is the first major painting of Brewster's career. It is an uncompromising and intensely lyrical statement about the artist's love of colour and his forceful requirement to express views about the natural world through the use of colour alone. It is a painting of intellectual and technical certainty.

7. *The Garden and House at Kingston Lacy.*
Charcoal on paper
1990. 28 × 36

There is, then, a new depth of feeling within Brewster's mature work in the 1980s. Each painting may start from the notion of a systematic organisation of colour in the chosen canvas or series of canvases, but a move can be identified from the more overtly structured paintings from the beginning of the period (such as *Barbary* and *Pale Light*, 1983, ill.27,28). These are perhaps less than satisfactory works, since the blocks of colour either in a pale palette or in the more intensely coloured canvas in *Barbary* seem to jostle rather uncomfortably against each other. Each canvas has a slightly jarred feeling. This was largely the result of working in a small studio in the artist's house and was also a consequence of using acrylics rather than oils because of the limited studio conditions. Brewster discovered the way of synthesising areas of colour throughout this period and giving the whole canvas its energy and focus, without compromising on the collision of colour within each individual work. The paintings lose their more literal influence of Hofmann. Some canvases which rely on a heavy concentration of graded areas of deep red hint at Mark Rothko's paintings for the Four Seasons Restaurant in the Seagram

Building, New York, gifted to the Tate Gallery in 1968-69. Brewster's deep commitment in his painting to give visible form to states of emotion, continues to have its roots in a formal representational understanding of the natural world. His developing body of work contains, and continues to contain, studies of landscapes which genuinely reflect his observations of specific places. A work such as *Blue Pool* from 1982 can be read as an abstracted view of a literal place in nature, or as a purely abstract work. All of these works from the first half of the decade are underpinned by energetic and literal drawings of landscapes. Printmaking too becomes an important outcome of Brewster's work, providing an attractive counterpoint to the profusion of acrylic and oil paintings of this period. His method of working – often listening to carefully selected extracts of music in the studio – emphasises the values of organisation, discipline and order as prerequisites for inspiration and painterly drama.

Brewster's work sits confidently and authoritatively in the space between romanticism and formal abstraction. The artist is happy to work both literally and metaphorically. That space between nature and the abstraction of nature is for him the most intensely creative space. What gives his work its coherence is that passionate involvement with uncompromising colour derived from his student paintings, which remains with the artist to this day.

Brewster moved away from the use of acrylic in the early 1980s because, whilst it enabled him to paint with speed and vigour, the concluding results lacked the depth and texture which only oil paint could bring. The return to working purely in oil was to mark the authentic beginnings of Brewster's mature style and with it the beginnings of his commercial success. Critical attention gained momentum during this period, crystallised by important exhibitions in 1986; a solo show at the Winchester School of Art, and the exhibition 'The Group of Four' at the Warwick Art Trust, which built on Brewster's involvement in 'English Expressionism', held at the same London gallery in 1984.

'English Expressionism' was a defining exhibition for him. It was a large-scale survey of leading British Abstract Expressionists and brought him into professional contact with prestigious and renowned artists such as John Hoyland, Gillian Ayres, Bert Irvin and John Walker. Though he had been invited to show at the very last moment, Brewster gained an influential London audience, as well as serious critical attention, resulting in an invitation to hold a solo show at the Warwick Arts Trust in 1985.

Corinna Lotz, arts critic of *Newsline*, introduced 'The Group of Four' exhibition at the Warwick Arts Trust in 1986 by indicating 'the artists' common interest in painterly quality and a heightened understanding of the power of colour which sets them apart from the present preoccupation with the return to figuration which has been hailed as the main feature of painting in the 1980s. All of them have a very strong sense of their debt to the work of the New York school of Abstract Expressionism, but they are rapidly developing and expanding the discoveries of their predecessors'. The artists concerned, Brewster, Sheila Girling, Donnagh McKenna and Viacheslav Atroshenko, showed lyrical, abstract paintings of a particular energy and vibrancy. In fact Brewster's work in this show (one important oil, *Deep Down*, ill.36, and five acrylic works) seemed comparatively subdued, though they were certainly not introspective.

Deep Down is a particularly important painting. It occupies the space between a real and an imagined natural place. The canvas shows what could be the surface of an intense pool or seascape, using the same combination of deep indigo blues and a paler blue

which characterised *Above and Beyond* from the same year. But the hurried and agitated flecks of red, yellow and white which scurry across the surface of this painting do not indicate natural forms, but rather express the inner turbulence of the scene and perhaps a sense of the life within the pool. This is a painting about what lies beneath the surface of a natural place. It is a compelling and articulate image. The painting demonstrates the possibilities of a fluid and lyrical style which could only be achieved by working in oil.

The acrylic paintings for 'The Group of Four' show were harder and edgier. Works such as *River Run* demonstrate the coldness and chill of a fast-moving mountain stream. *Heart of Darkness* attempted to encapsulate the brooding essence of Joseph Conrad's novel, and offers a bridge to the *Beauty and Sadness* series of the 1990s. Brewster does not attempt to extract any single meaning from these works. They are highly personal statements about real or imagined places, and their ambiguity creates depth and mystery in lyrical beauty for the viewer.

8. *St Aldhelm's Head.*
Charcoal on paper 1990.
28 × 36 p/c

In 1986, Brewster held a defining solo exhibition at Winchester School of Art. The show, hung in the cool white formal expanse of the art gallery at the School, demonstrated the range of Brewster's achievement. The large oil *In the Garden* (ill.32) is one of the sparest of his paintings to date. It shows, perhaps, the effect of heavy rain on a well-known landscape for Brewster, his parents' garden. But there is nothing of the physical evidence of a garden within this canvas, rather the sense of the vitality of natural colour sharpened and made more liquid by a covering of heavy rain. The painting is about the strength and vital force of nature. Brewster has found that strength and vitality, unusually, with a sparse canvas. There are a number of other works in the 1980s which rely on a lighter palette, though these seem to be somehow less successfully handled. Pale colour, though handled authoritatively in a work such as *Early Light* (ill.31), does not carry the full force of Brewster's conviction. It is perhaps not surprising that his best work from 1986 onwards rarely relies on this cooler palette, or this sparse understatement.

John Gillett, in a sensitive essay on Brewster's work for the catalogue for the Winchester exhibition, carefully described the typical process of a Brewster painting. 'He does not work towards a vision of the completed painting, but paints from certain starting points, primarily of a formal nature: the size and format of the canvas; some notion of the area of colour and tonality within which the painting is to develop; or simply a feeling of, say light or darkness, or richness; or a structural consideration, such as an emphasis on the horizontal or vertical. The choice of such starting points is influenced by the nature of work just finished and by the direction of other paintings in progress. Brewster usually works on a number of canvases concurrently, and each painting may take several months to complete'.

Brewster's ability to see a range of paintings in his mind's eye, and develop the complex idea of a series of works on similar colour themes, as well as his ability to build narrative strength into his diptych and triptychs, were viewed by other critics of the period as evidence of a new toughness and intellectual rigour. Increasingly, collectors of his work – and his client list extended from individuals through to major corporate purchases in this period – reacted enthusiastically both to the exhilarating hot, wet, colour intensely worked on to these canvases, as well as to the clear intellectual rationale which underpinned the works.

In 1983, Brewster moved to a new studio in Hackney, and concentrated on oil painting as a preferred medium, working on bigger canvases. But the sense of the need for the internal structure and organisation of each painting, whatever its size or scale, remained strongly with him. His large paintings, as well as the most successful of his smaller works, are concerned with intense panoramic space, a remarkable natural place contained beyond the boundaries of each individual painting. It was this compelling effect, the journey that a painting could take one to, that finally broke Brewster's early reliance in the 1980s on a simple oppositional use of blocks of colour. And it is because these journeys refer ultimately to a natural or imagined place, that they have their strength and vitality. This ambiguous place between the abstract and representational is the heartland of Brewster's œuvre. What holds firm is the lyrical, expressive and passionate use of colour, and the honed ability to organise a canvas in a compelling and yet highly allusive manner.

Brewster's print work in the 1980s shows the same facility and energy. He was particularly interested in using the silkscreen monoprint format, enabling him to create

unique works of art very much in the style of his oil painting. Brewster was particularly keen to use the print medium to articulate his views about producing extended series of paintings on similar colour themes. The profusion in printmaking in this period demonstrates a long-term programme and remarkable concentration. After struggling to achieve the kind of result in printmaking he wanted, a breakthrough came in 1986 when he started to use an 'open' screen and a much more immediate and spontaneous way of handling the coloured inks, effectively painting and drawing directly through the screen and building up the printed image as he would a painting. No longer restricted to producing editions of identical prints, he embarked on producing almost endless series of related silkscreen monoprints, a process which continues to this day.

Recent work

Martyn Brewster's series of oil paintings and prints *Beauty and Sadness* marked a decisive moment in the artist's career. Conceived in 1995 and the subject of a major show at the Jill George Gallery in London during the following year, the work explored the dramatic and emotional possibilities of placing deep areas of black at the heart of otherwise in-

9. Coastline.
Ink and wash 1993.
8 × 11

tensely coloured work. In a characteristic screenprint from this series, *Beauty and Sadness No.30* (ill.66), the vividness of the central black area of colour at the heart of the print is startling in its profundity. This is a journey we have seen in Brewster's early work from the 1970s and 1980s where a central area of darkness has been the focus from which other brighter colours extend. There is a new hardness to this series, a new and sombre reflectiveness, as well as an aggressiveness never before seen in Brewster's work. This *Beauty and Sadness* print has a jazzy abstraction about it which belies the sombre heart of the work. The deep black core of the painting on close inspection is in itself textured with a glossy layer overlying a more sombre heart, which in turn modulates to the very deepest blue at the edges of the work. The print is contained by the most startling and vivid red blocks of colour overscored with harsh downward lines. It is not a comfortable work. It has the hallmark of organisation, composure and certainty which is character-istic of Brewster's best work but it shows a more troubled and perhaps even pessimistic mood, brought about partly by a desire to broaden the imagery in the paintings, and partly as a response to the increasing unhappiness in his personal life.

The *Beauty and Sadness* series shows Brewster's work at its most evocative. It shows that within the supposed constraints of lyrical colour painting, the artist can find new directions, new purpose and new meaning. This authoritative quest, throughout the work of the 1990s, signifies paintings of importance as well as maturity. Such a work is typical of his authority as an artist. The ability to see the manifestations of an image through a coherent and individualistic series of works, whether in the medium of print, the artist's book or the oil painting, is a tribute both to the breadth of his vision and the desire to work out the totality of a creative idea. The 1990s have seen an extraordinary flourishing of his art.

In 1989 Brewster took up a post as visiting lecturer at the Bournemouth and Poole College of Art and Design (a position he still holds) and in 1990 moved to Bourne-mouth. One of the first artistic signals of this change in personal circumstances was a series of landscape drawings in charcoal on paper, or ink and wash on paper, which Brewster drew throughout 1990. He saw this project as an opportunity to familiarise himself with new domestic surroundings as well as to get a grounding in his new location in Bournemouth and on the Dorset coast. This series was shown in an exhi-bition which toured to museums and galleries along the South coast, including showings at the Russell-Cotes Art Gallery and Museum in Bournemouth, the Dorset County Museum in Dorchester, with two showings at private dealers, the Jill George Gallery in London and the On Line Gallery in Southampton. For an artist whose reputation had been principally built on the strength of his lyrical abstract paintings, this exhibition came as something of a surprise, a convincing essay in the representation of landscape. The landscape is clearly of real and known places, Bournemouth Bay in the afternoon, the garden and house at Kingston Lacy, drawings of Hengistbury Head in Bournemouth and St Aldhelm's Head on the Isle of Purbeck.

Whilst the drawings are literal in the sense that, to a local observer, they clearly repre-sent familiar scenes, the drawings have an epic sweep too. There is a joyous skill in the depiction of light reflecting on water, and transfusing the whole feeling of the drawing. And if these are known places, then there is one surprising feature to them: they are landscapes without people. They represent the geographical and atmospheric circum-stances in what is customarily a densely populated landscape, in a completely natural

setting. Brewster is not interested in human transgression or buildings impinging upon nature (apart from the literal studies of Kingston Lacy House, which is drawn in a more organic way as if it had grown literally out of the landscape). He is describing geographical locations to emphasise the timeless and permanent strength of nature. These drawings have the same importance to Brewster as the series of paintings of his parents' garden in the 1980s, serving to fix his attention in a particular place, give guidance to a future programme of work, and test his skill in a mode in which he had not shown to the public before.

An exhibition of charcoal and ink and wash drawings would not have been what most people would have expected Brewster to undertake as his first project in the 1990s. The vitality and energy of the drawings, however, show the artist completely at home in his chosen medium, and remind us how essential drawing has been to Brewster's abstract art. It is perhaps the artist's own recognition of this fact that led him, in these mature drawings, to dedicate the works and the exhibition to Dennis Creffield, his early art school tutor. For the exhibition at the Russell-Cotes Art Gallery and Museum, Bournemouth

10. *Coastline series*, No.3.
Etching ed.60 1993. 6 × 8

('The Land and the Sea,' a two-person show with Abi Kremer in 1993) Brewster also displayed the commanding triptych, *Sea and Sky* (ill.41), now in the gallery's permanent collections. The relationship between the Russell-Cotes and the artist was strongly forged at this time. A major consequence proved to be the retrospective exhibition 'Martyn Brewster' curated by Simon Olding and Mark Bills and held at the Russell-Cotes Art Gallery and Museum in the summer of 1997.

The concentration of printmaking work throughout the 1990s has been a feature of Brewster's mature art. Two printmaking awards, for the artist to study at the Lowick House print shop in the Lake District in 1994 and 1996, also focused the artist's attention on this medium. During his residencies at Lowick House, the artist made full use of the screenprint studio, producing hundreds of prints and a number of folded silk-screenprinted books, often working out singular ideas in abstract colour in extended series of prints. The artist's books encapsulate the essence of the repetitive but individual series of prints by giving them one common integrated form. He sees the folded concertina-style books as a run of images working in collaboration to illuminate a single theme. These artist's books are perhaps his closest attempt to turn the visual arts into a form of 'concrete poetry' simultaneously exploring the possibilities of abstraction through the organised response to nature. Certainly the Lowick residencies, and the resultant body of work, draw from a direct response to nature and his emotional reaction to the particular geographic circumstances of the Lake District.

These prints and books have the sparse direct elegance characteristic of Brewster's work, which makes in some ways the Bournemouth landscape drawings even more remarkable for the gentleness of their evocation of familiar landscapes and the subtle and rounded coastline of Dorset. Perhaps Brewster is responding to the sense of an historic 'Wessex' rather than contemporary Bournemouth. As in the Lowick prints, which are not based on a particular place but rather evoke the mood and complexity of nature, the Bournemouth drawings refer to the notion of a prehistoric landscape, where the artist is drawn by the strange remoteness of the beach without tourists, piers or seaside buildings. He is interested in the depiction of nature, geography and archaeology, not the 'damage' inflicted by a human presence. Most of all he is affected by physical beauty, and the abundance of shape, line, colour, texture and climatic changes.

The work of the 1990s shows Brewster's characteristic determination to create art out of the very essence of nature. He does not seek to reproduce directly what is seen but to reflect on the occasion and presence of a natural moment. Three important shows during this decade demonstrate the creative profusion of Brewster's mature abstract art. 'Light Fall' was an exhibition of paintings and monotypes at the Thumb Gallery, directed by Jill George in Soho, London in 1990. The signature work of the exhibition, *Light Fall* (ill.35), is a free expression of the sometimes dazzling effect of light on water. The notion of light reflecting off the surface leads to the formal structure of the painting, with an intense blue leading to a white area commanding the right-hand side of the canvas, and the surface of water emphasised in a deeper blue palette to the left-hand side. Both areas are drawn together by the spillover of white paint across the canvas in a turbulent and heavily worked surface.

A companion piece, *Night Fall* (ill.37), is a more literal evocation of a natural scene, this time with a brooding, intense, deep blue colour suffusing the entire canvas, with only smaller areas picked out with the lightest traces of yellow or red paint fluttering

11. *Bournemouth Bay, afternoon sunlight*. Charcoal on paper 1992. 30 × 22½

across the surface of the image. *Evening Shadows* (ill.40) shows Brewster's commanding use of red blocks of colour to create a powerful image. Again the canvas is divided into two distinct areas. Deep red blocks and areas of worked colour sitting at the base of the painting are transmuted into the upper half where the red almost disappears into a profoundly black central area. This is not a painting which refers to any particular place; it is entirely an effect of rich, romantic mood. Brewster showed in this series an earlier work from 1988, *Winter Light* (triptych, ill.38). This was by now an unusual excursion into a lighter and more chilling palette, and is perhaps the most successful of Brewster's works in near monochrome. Due to the use of the triptych form, the internal narrative of the painting, which describes the passage of a huge snow storm over cold grey ground, gives the work its meaning and coherence. These big nature paintings show an artist working at the peak of his capabilities. They are romantic evocations of nature expressed in purely abstract or nearly abstract forms. They show Brewster working in his most creative mode in his chosen area between figuration and abstraction. There is no compromise in this space, only the vigour, intellectual and technical control of the artist.

One of the most important creative partnerships that Brewster has developed throughout his career has been the relationship with Jill George, his London dealer, who has given him regular one person shows at her gallery in Soho; such was an exhibition of paintings and monoprints in 1992 which showed Brewster in his most optimistic vein. Many of his larger oils for this exhibition, with their composition formed of a series of abstract small blocks of deep blues and reds, show the hint of the beginnings of this form dating back to his earliest oil paintings in the 1970s and 1980s. But here the handling was altogether freer, more expressive and more coherent. The canvas was seen as a powerful organising force bearing down on these encroaching and luminous areas of colour. There was a consistency and unity to each painting which escaped the artist's earliest works in this medium.

The most successful works were smaller canvases where Brewster showed a 'variation' series (ill.42-45) with strident, aggressively worked blocks of colour in small canvases working harmoniously with and beside each other. If these works had a tendency to be purely decorative, then this is not to deny their expressive impact. They showed Brewster working competently and with high technical skill across a planned series of works on a similar colour theme. The creation of one work led inevitably to the possibility of another, giving each individual variation series their proximity of relationship, as well as the possibility of expansion of the single idea. Even within the single series or variations of works, one had the sense that the artist was beginning to think about the next programmed series of paintings. The silk-screen monoprints in this exhibition were amongst the most successful that Brewster has ever undertaken. The prints with, unusually, ragged edges, contain rich and lyrical areas of colour, often with one luminous closely worked side to the print in deep orange, reds, yellows or blues reflecting a darker and more sombre side to the print. The sense of the opposites working against each other gives each print its dynamic vigour. They have the same force and the same conviction as the small and larger oil paintings within this series.

The optimism and the self-evident exuberance of Brewster's paintings, is then, a defining characteristic, and it has been imaginatively explored during the 1990s. However, a significant change was to take place in Brewster's exhibition *Beauty and Sadness* for the Jill George Gallery in the summer of 1996. This exhibition contained the harder edged

30

and jazzier prints described at the outset of this chapter but it is with the large oil paintings in the *Beauty and Sadness* series that Brewster makes his most intense poetic statements. Gone, in the majority of these works, is the lyrical and passionate area of rich colour at the heart of the abstract work. It has been replaced by a brooding area of black or intense darkness. Even in the most luminous paintings in this series there is a darker heart, an encroaching area of black paint which moves inevitably into the centre of each square canvas. The large diptych in the *Beauty and Sadness* series emphasises this point most dramatically. There is a black expanse at the centre of the painting pressing insistently and vigorously out against the deeply grained and brighter red and blues which are at the edge of both square canvases. Yet, as in his prints, the paint surface is more complex and subtle. Because the paint surface is so intensely worked, shades and contours of this deep void give subtle suggestions of reflected colour. The brush details within this black heart are also evident, drawing attention to the artist in the physical process of making the art. In these paintings, then, black is not a colour, but the originator of colour. Whilst the heart of these paintings may, on initial impact, be seen to be simply dead, a void, an area of non-colour, they cannot operate without colour. Colour comes from black.

12. *Studland from Hengistbury Head.* Charcoal on paper 1992. 14 × 20

31

This is a more melancholy, introspective and a tougher form of painting. The *Beauty and Sadness* diptych is perhaps the most introspective work that Brewster has ever painted. Only at the spare edges of this major painting does colour transform the work. The saturated scored red and blue have been pushed to the very extremity of the canvas, as if almost not there at all. This is a painting about despair. It only just hints at the possibility of that despair being transfigured by the luminous all-embracing power of colour. It is as if Brewster has reviewed his entire artistic career, his entire artistic belief in the power of colour, and for a moment, found that power wanting. This is a moment of chilling insight, and perhaps the most personal statement that Brewster could have made. It is a painting about the possibility of his art failing. This sense of failure, which has become a commentary on Brewster's life and work, is astonishingly frank and revelatory. And yet he used this highly important exhibition to work a moral abyss. The series contains other powerful works which transfigure or mitigate the deep uncertainty caused by looking into blackness. *Beauty and Sadness* No. 5 (ill. 51), for example, continues the theme of darkness at the heart of creation. The vividly red, orange and deep blue edges of the canvas show stirrings of the poetic life which give the canvas its balance and mitigates its pessimism. Other works in the series, such as *Fading Sunset* (ill. 47), are more literal workings of Brewster's chosen area towards figuration. They have all of the poetry and lyricism which one anticipates from his mature handling of paint.

Brewster himself remarks on this most important exhibition that: 'the nature paintings continue to reflect a more overt concern with movement and light, the world out there, whereas the new series of works in this exhibition reflect a quieter meditative and melancholy concern. I hope, however, their stillness is suffused with atmosphere and vibrant with longing. In essence all the works are celebratory whether or not they are more concerned with an intense interest in what we see "out there" or what we feel "inside".' His comments hint at personal turmoil, and indeed Brewster's marriage had broken up by this time.

These introspective, dark paintings take the viewer into rare areas of self-reflection. This is an unusual place for the admirer of Brewster's dynamic colour paintings to be. There is a harder abstract world here, a tougher world but one in which even from the darkest place inner colour will eventually suffuse and give meaning to the canvas. We are forced to look deep into these dark shadows but we find that colour is eventually triumphant and that the despairing mood of melancholy can be journeyed both through and beyond.

This emotional and artistic journey has carried Brewster through to a joyous and celebratory group of prints from his residency at Lowick in September 1996. These are screenprints of splendid energy and rich sumptuous colour. Using a square paper format, glowing bands of blue, shades of yellow-orange, red and occasionally green are worked into the print. They are works of optimism, open celebrations of the evocative power of colour. Whilst they maintain the hallmarks of Brewster's mature style – carefully organised, glowing in colour – there is a vitality, spontaneity and near abandon here which gives each print its forceful individuality. They demonstrate the artist's remarkable capacity to work within a carefully chosen area, and to discover inexhaustible variations and fresh reworkings of a deeply serious theme.

13. *Untitled*. Oil on canvas 1968-69. 33 × 16

14. *Still life*. Oil on canvas 1971. 12 × 9½   15. *Portrait of Anthony Beale*. Oil on board 1971. 16 × 12

16. *Grandmother*. Oil on canvas 1971. 28 × 20

17. *Bedroom in Brighton*. Oil on canvas 1971. 17 × 22½

18. *The Blossom Trees*. Oil on canvas 1971. 14 × 10

19. *Portrait of Mark Gallagher.* Oil on canvas 1972. 30 × 27

20. *Reclining nude*. Oil on canvas 1972. 24 × 24

21. *Daffodils*. Oil on board 1972. 21½ × 19¾

22. *Self-portrait*. Oil on canvas 1972. 17 × 15½

23. *Line of moving figures*. Oil on canvas 1973. 59 × 47

24. *Autumn*. Oil on canvas 1974. 60 × 48

25. *Self-portrait*. Oil on canvas 1976. 16 × 12

26. *Self-portrait*. Acrylic on canvas 1977. 30 × 24

27. *Barbary*. Acrylic on canvas 1983. 72×96

28. *Pale Light*. Acrylic on canvas 1983. 77 × 68

29. *Night Garden*. Oil on canvas 1976. 37 × 48

30. *In the sky*. Oil on canvas 1985. 62 × 36

31. *Early Light*. Oil on canvas 1986. 72 × 60

32. *In the Garden*. Oil on canvas 1986. 72 × 60

33. *Above and Beyond*, triptych. Oil on canvas 1986. 96 × 156

34. *Scent of Rain*. Oil on canvas 1986. 72 × 60

35. *Light Fall*. Oil on canvas 1990. 72 × 60

36. *Deep Down*. Oil on canvas 1986. 69 × 90

37. *Night Fall*. Oil on canvas 1988. 72 × 60

38. *Winter Light*, triptych. Oil on canvas 1988. 96 × 156

39. *Ocean Light* 1. Oil on canvas 1990. 54 × 46

40. *Evening Shadows*. Oil on canvas 1990. 72 × 60

41. *Sea and Sky*, triptych No.2. Oil on canvas 1991. 72 × 134

42. *Variation series*, No.8. Oil on canvas 1992. 12 × 10

43. *Variation series*, No.10. Oil on canvas 1992. 12 × 10

44. *Variation series*, No.11. Oil on canvas 1992. 12 × 10

45. *Variation series*, No.9. Oil on canvas 1992. 12 × 10

46. *Wildfire* square variations, series no.55. Oil on canvas 1994. 14 × 14

47. *Fading Sunset*. Oil on canvas 1996. 76 × 76

48. *Beauty and Sadness*, No.2. Oil on canvas 1996. 76 × 76

49

50

49. *Night and Day* (diptych). Oil on canvas 1994. 76 × 152
50. *Beauty and Sadness*, diptych. Oil on canvas 1996. 76 × 15271

51. *Beauty and Sadness*, No.5. Oil on canvas 1996. 60 × 60

52. *Beauty and Sadness*, No.10. Oil on canvas 1996. 48 × 48

53

54

53. *Celebration*. Silkscreen monoprint 1992. 16 × 30
54. *Red Glow*. Silkscreen monoprint 1992. 16 × 30

55. *Lowick*, No.70. Silkscreen monoprint 1994. 23 × 23

56. *Lowick*, No.100. Silkscreen monoprint 1995. 14 × 14

57. *Lowick*, No.451. Silkscreen monoprint 1996. 23 × 23

58. *Lowick*, No.452. Silkscreen monoprint 1996. 23 × 23

59. *Lowick*, No.457. Silkscreen monoprint 1996. 23 × 23

60. *Lowick*, No.454. Silkscreen monoprint 1996. 23 × 23

61. *Lowick*, No.453. Silkscreen monoprint 1996. 23 × 23

62. *Lowick*, No.456. Silkscreen monoprint 1996. 23 × 23

63. *Lowick*, No.450. Silkscreen monoprint 1996. 23 × 23

64. *Beauty and Sadness*, Variation No.1. Oil on canvas 1996. 14 × 14

65. *Beauty and Sadness*, No.51. Silkscreen monoprint 1996. 17 × 17

66. *Beauty and Sadness*, No.30. Silkscreen monoprint 1996. 17 × 17

67. *Beauty and Sadness*, No.50. Silkscreen monoprint 1996. 17 × 17

68. *Beauty and Sadness*, No.52. Silkscreen monoprint 1996. 17 × 17

69. *Beauty and Sadness*. Collograph 1996. 23 × 23

70

71

70. *Lightfall*, No.1. Artist proof. Etching ed.60 1996. 4 × 4
71. *Lightfall*, No.2. Artist proof. Etching ed.60 1996. 4 × 4

72. *First Light*. Artist proof. Collograph 1996. 10 × 10

Illustrations

All dimensions are in inches, height before width. Works whose titles are followed by an asterisk are in private collections, with the exception of 4, 10 and 41 which are in the collection of the Russell-Cotes Art Gallery and Museum.

1. *Standing figure*. Charcoal on paper 1971. 23 × 16½
2. *Seated nude*. Charcoal on paper 1972. 30½ × 20½
3. *Garden, Hertfordshire*. Charcoal on paper 1973. 30 × 20
4. *Garden series, No.4 (The tall tree).*★ Etching ed.60 1993. 8 × 6
5. *Devil's Dyke, Sussex*. Ink pen and wash 1978. 11½ × 16
6. *Welsh landscape*. Ink and wash 1985. 12 × 17
7. *The Garden and House at Kingston Lacy*. Charcoal on paper 1990. 28 × 36
8. *St Aldhelm's Head*.★ Charcoal on paper 1990. 28 × 36 p/c
9. *Coastline*. Ink and wash 1993. 8 × 11
10. *Coastline series, No.3*.★ Etching ed.60 1993. 6 × 8
11. *Bournemouth Bay, afternoon sunlight*. Charcoal on paper 1992. 30 × 22½
12. *Studland from Hengistbury Head*. Charcoal on paper 1992. 14 × 20
13. *Untitled*. Oil on canvas 1968-69. 33 × 16
14. *Still life*. Oil on canvas 1971. 12 × 9½
15. *Portrait of Anthony Beale*. Oil on board 1971. 16 × 12
16. *Grandmother*. Oil on canvas 1971. 28 × 20
17. *Bedroom in Brighton*. Oil on canvas 1971. 17 × 22½
18. *The Blossom Trees*. Oil on canvas 1971. 14 × 10
19. *Portrait of Mark Gallagher*. Oil on canvas 1972. 30 × 27
20. *Reclining nude*. Oil on canvas 1972. 24 × 24
21. *Daffodils*. Oil on board 1972. 21½ × 19¾
22. *Self-portrait*. Oil on canvas 1972. 17 × 15½
23. *Line of moving figures*. Oil on canvas 1973. 59 × 47
24. *Autumn*. Oil on canvas 1974. 60 × 48
25. *Self-portrait*. Oil on canvas 1976. 16 × 12
26. *Self-portrait*. Acrylic on canvas 1977. 30 × 24
27. *Barbary*. Acrylic on canvas 1983. 72 × 96
28. *Pale Light*. Acrylic on canvas 1983. 77 × 68
29. *Night Garden*. Oil on canvas 1976. 37 × 48
30. *In the sky*.★ Oil on canvas 1985. 62 × 36
31. *Early Light*. Oil on canvas 1986. 72 × 60
32. *In the Garden*.★ Oil on canvas 1986. 72 × 60
33. *Above and Beyond*, triptych. Oil on canvas 1986. 96 × 156
34. *Scent of Rain*.★ Oil on canvas 1986. 72 × 60
35. *Light Fall*. Oil on canvas 1990. 72 × 60
36. *Deep Down*.★ Oil on canvas 1986. 69 × 90
37. *Night Fall*. Oil on canvas 1988. 72 × 60
38. *Winter Light*, triptych. Oil on canvas 1988. 96 × 156
39. *Ocean Light 1*.★ Oil on canvas 1990. 54 × 46
40. *Evening Shadows*.★ Oil on canvas 1990. 72 × 60
41. *Sea and Sky*, triptych No.2.★ Oil on canvas 1991. 72 × 134
42-45. *Variation series*, Nos 8-11.★ Oil on canvas 1992. 12 × 10
46. *Wildfire* square variations, series no.55.★ Oil on canvas 1994. 14 × 14
47. *Fading Sunset*. Oil on canvas 1996. 76 × 76
48. *Beauty and Sadness, No.2*. Oil on canvas 1996. 76 × 76
49. *Night and Day* (diptych).★ Oil on canvas 1994. 76 × 152
50. *Beauty and Sadness*, diptych. Oil on canvas 1996. 76 × 152
51. *Beauty and Sadness, No.5*.★ Oil on canvas 1996. 60 × 60
52. *Beauty and Sadness, No.10*.★ Oil on canvas 1996. 48 × 48
53. *Celebration*.★ Silkscreen monoprint 1992. 16 × 30
54. *Red Glow*.★ Silkscreen monoprint 1992. 16 × 30
55. *Lowick, No.70*. Silkscreen monoprint 1994. 23 × 23
56. *Lowick, No.100*. Silkscreen monoprint 1995. 14 × 14
57. *Lowick, No.451*. Silkscreen monoprint 1996. 23 × 23
58. *Lowick, No.452*. Silkscreen monoprint 1996. 23 × 23
59. *Lowick, No.457*. Silkscreen monoprint 1996. 23 × 23
60. *Lowick, No.454*. Silkscreen monoprint 1996. 23 × 23
61. *Lowick, No.453*. Silkscreen monoprint 1996. 23 × 23
62. *Lowick, No.456*. Silkscreen monoprint 1996. 23 × 23
63. *Lowick, No.450*.★ Silkscreen monoprint 1996. 23 × 23
64. *Beauty and Sadness*, Variation No.1.★ Oil on canvas 1996. 14 × 14
65. *Beauty and Sadness, No.51*. Silkscreen monoprint 1996. 17 × 17
66. *Beauty and Sadness, No.30*.★ Silkscreen monoprint 1996. 17 × 17
67. *Beauty and Sadness, No.50*. Silkscreen monoprint 1996. 17 × 17
68. *Beauty and Sadness, No.52*. Silkscreen monoprint 1996. 17 × 17
69. *Beauty and Sadness*. Collograph 1996. 23 × 23
70. *Lightfall*, No.1. Artist proof. Etching ed.60 1996. 4 × 4
71. *Lightfall*, No.2. Artist proof. Etching ed.60 1996. 4 × 4
72. *First Light*. Artist proof. Collograph 1996. 10 × 10

Biography

1952
Born in Oxford

1970-71
Hertfordshire College of Art and Design

1971-74
Brighton Polytechnic, BA Fine Art (Painting): first-class honours

1974-75
Brighton Polytechnic, Postgraduate Printmaking Diploma: distinction

1977
Eastern Arts Award

1977-78
Art Teacher's Certificate, Sussex University

1979-80
Art Teacher, Bedfords Park Comprehensive School, Essex

1980-89
Lecturer in Art, East Hertfordshire College
Visiting Lecturer, Winchester School of Art

1983-92
Working in SPACE studio, London

1989-
Visiting Lecturer, Bournemouth & Poole College of Art and Design

1990
Moved to Bournemouth

1991
British Council Award to exhibit in USA

1992
Bournemouth Arts Grant, Bournemouth Borough Council

1994
Openshaw Printmaking Award, Lowick House Print Workshop, Cumbria

1995
Arts Council of England, Development Grant

1996
Robert Horne Printmaking Award, Lowick House Print Workshop, Cumbria

Selected solo exhibitions

1977
Watford Centre Library Gallery, Hertfordshire
Hertfordshire College of Art (two person)

1982
Harlow Playhouse Gallery, Essex
Hornsey Library Gallery, London

1983
Peterborough City Museum and Art Gallery
Letchworth Museum and Art Gallery

1984
Bury St Edmunds Art Gallery, Suffolk
London College of Furniture

1985
Brighton Polytechnic (two person)
Wilmer, Cutler and Pickering, Law Associates, London

1986
Warwick Arts Trust, London
Winchester Gallery, Winchester School of Art
Minories Art Gallery, Exeter

1987
Woodlands Art Gallery, London

1988
'Shadows and Light', Thumb Gallery, London
Bede Gallery, Jarrow

1989
Thumb Gallery, London (two person)

1990
'Light Falls', Thumb Gallery, London

1991
Atlanta '91 (Jill George Gallery), USA

1992
Jill George Gallery, London

1993
Upstairs Gallery, Upton Country Park, Dorset
Pallant House, Chichester
'The Land and the Sea', Russell-Cotes Art Gallery and Museum,
Bournemouth (with Abi Kremer)
On Line Gallery, Southampton
'New works on paper', Jill George Gallery, London

1994
Dorset County Museum, Dorchester
Jill George Gallery, London
Contema Strichting, Netherlands

1995
'Monoprints from Lowick',
Jill George Gallery, London

1996
'Beauty and Sadness',
Jill George Gallery, London
On Line Gallery, Southampton

1997
Russell-Cotes Art Gallery and Museum, Bournemouth
'Works on paper', Coram Gallery, London
'Recent Prints', Jill George Gallery, London

Selected group exhibitions

1974
Stowells Trophy, Mall Galleries, London

1975
Brighton Specialist Printmakers, Oxford University Press, London
Brighton Printmakers, Gardner Art Centre, Sussex

1983
Royal Festival Hall, London

1984
'English Expressionism', Warwick Arts Trust, London

1985
Angela Flowers Gallery, London
Warwick Arts Trust, London
Bede Gallery, Jarrow

1986
'The Group of Four', Warwick Arts Trust, London
Peterborough Art Gallery – Visual Hire Scheme Tour

1987
'First Showings Take Two', Thumb Gallery, London
369 Gallery, Edinburgh

1988
Warwick Arts Trust Collection, London
'Romantic Visions', Camden Arts Centre, London
London Group, 75th Anniversary Exhibition, RCA, London

1989
'5 Abstract Artists', Thumb Gallery, London
Art LA 1989, Los Angeles, USA (Thumb Gallery)
Critics Choice, Air Gallery, London
Bede Gallery, Jarrow
Ianetti Landzone Gallery, San Francisco, USA

Selected public and corporate collections

1990
Art London (Thumb Gallery)
'London to Atlanta', Atlanta, USA (Thumb Gallery)
'The Drawing Show II', Thumb Gallery
5th Art LA, Los Angeles, USA (Thumb Gallery)

1991
Decouvertes, Paris, France (Jill George Gallery)
6th Art LA, Los Angeles, USA (Jill George Gallery)
'Small is Beautiful', Angela Flowers Gallery, London
On Line Gallery, Southampton

1992
Art 92, London (Jill George Gallery)
ARCO 92, Madrid, Spain (Jill George Gallery)
On Line Gallery, Southampton
Dorset Art Week, Athelhampton House, Dorset
7th Art LA, Los Angeles, USA (Jill George Gallery)

1993
Art 93, London (Jill George Gallery)
Decouvertes, Paris, France (Jill George Gallery)
Los Angeles International, USA (Jill George Gallery)
On Line Gallery, Southampton
Chicago Art Fair, USA (Jill George Gallery)
Ohio, USA (Jill George Gallery)

1994
Art 94, London (Jill George Gallery)
CAS Market, London
On Line Gallery, Southampton

1995
Art 95, London (Jill George Gallery)
FIAC, Paris
'The Drawing Show III', Jill George Gallery, London
On Line Gallery, Southampton

1996
Art 96, London, Jill George Gallery
Gallery Ellison Marshall, Bordeaux
On Line Gallery, Southampton
Glasgow Art Fair, Jill George Gallery
CAS, Royal Festival Hall, London
Monoprints from Jill George Gallery, Gainsborough House,
Suffolk

1997
3rd British International Miniature Print exhibition (travelling)
Rubicon Gallery, Dublin
Art 97, Jill George Gallery

Bede Gallery, Jarrow
BMW (UK)
BUPA
Brighton Polytechnic
Cable and Wireless plc
Cambridge Institute of Education
Capital Initiatives
Central Japan Railway Co, Japan
Christiana Bank, London
East Hertfordshire College, Cheshunt
Emory University, USA
Epping Forest District Council
First Interstate Bank of California
Gartmore Investment Management
IBM (UK)
Land Securities
Logica Ltd
London Borough of Tower Hamlets
London Business School
London College of Furniture
Merck, Sharpe and Dohme
Mezzanine Management
Midland Bank plc
National Trust
NW Securities Bank
Paintings in Hospitals
Pallant House, Chichester
Peterborough Art Gallery
PIC Europe
Poole Museums Service
Robert Horne and Co Ltd
Russell-Cotes Art Gallery and Museum
St Thomas' Hospital
Sony Corporation
The Economist
The Open University
Tolman Cunard
Unilever plc
Warwick Arts Trust
Wilmer, Cutler and Pickering
Wiltshire County Council
Winchester Health Authority
Winchester School of Art

Martyn Brewster's work
is also held in many private collections
throughout the world.

Selected bibliography

1982
M. Hart, *Arts Review*, vol. 34, no. 15, 16 July

1983
M. Brewster, catalogue statement, Peterborough City Art Gallery
D. Holmes, *Peterborough Evening Telegraph*, 4 March
Interview for Radio Cambridge Arts Roundup

1984
P. Ward-Green, *Arts Review*, 25 May, review of 'English Expressionism', Warwick Arts Trust, London
A. Baillieu, *City Limits*, no. 138, 25 May, review of 'English Expressionism'
Critics Choice, Radio 3, 12 May, review of 'English Expressionism'
K. Patrick, introduction to exhibition catalogue, London College of Furniture

1985
Tim Dickson, *Financial Times*, 25 October
Larry Berryman, *Arts Review*, 8 November, review of show at Brighton Polytechnic

1986
C. Lotz, 'Group of Four' catalogue, Warwick Arts Trust, London.
J. Gillett, catalogue introduction, Winchester Gallery

1987
J. Norrie, *Arts Review*, 17 July, review of '5 Abstract Artists', Thumb Gallery
R. Jacques, *The Scotsman*, October, review of show at 369 Gallery, Edinburgh

1988
M. Rose Beaumont, *Arts Review*, 17 June, review of show at Thumb Gallery
G. Auty, *Spectator*, 13 August, review of 'Romantic Visions'
M. Wykes-Joyce, *Arts Review*, 9 September, review of Warwick Arts Trust Collection
Larry Berryman, *Arts Review*, 23 September, review of show at Terrace Gallery, Worthing
W. E. Johnson, *Northern Echo*, 30 September, review of show at Bede Gallery, Jarrow

1989
Guy Burn, *Arts Review*, 13 September, review of show at Thumb Gallery

1990
Keith Patrick, catalogue essay, Thumb Gallery.

1992
M. Brewster, catalogue statement, Jill George Gallery

1993
Keith Patrick, *The Landscape Drawings of Martyn Brewster*, travelling exhibition catalogue

1995
M. Brewster, 'New Monoprints and Folded Books', *Printmaking Today*, vol. 4, no. 4

1996
Simon Olding, catalogue introduction, *Beauty and Sadness*, Jill George Gallery
Jeremy Miles, *Bournemouth Evening Echo*, 11 June
Lynne Green, *Contemporary Art*, vol. 3, no. 3